D0707439

Nature Spirits:
Endangered Like the Bees

How Can We Help Them?

Elizabeth Wieting

New World Publications, LLC.

Copyright © 2009, New World Publications, LLC
PO Box 1413
Eugene, OR 97440
www.newworldpublication.com

ISBN # 978-0-615-30215-7

Table of Contents

1

INTRODUCTION

People are probably aware of the plight of the honey bees. News reports of the dying–off of bee colonies and of the predation of the viroa mite have been available for some time. It is sobering to realize that if many plant species aren't pollinated, they will also decline, and that in fact many of our food crops are dependent upon the activity of the bees.

But what is not so well known is that the well-being of the plant world is also dependent upon invisible helpers, the Nature Spirits of fairy tale and legend. Their situation is just as threatened as that of the bees. Our modern culture, which is permeating the world with its artificial materials and with the forces required to run its machines and electronic equipment, is producing an environment which is exceedingly difficult for them. The environments we produce are often so hostile to the invisible helpers in the nature kingdom that they are driven away, and their places taken by other beings less constructive in nature.

In the mid-1800s the American author Stephen Crane wrote a story which signaled a huge reversal of human consciousness. It was called _The Open Boat_, a story about people cast adrift from a sinking ship, trying to make their way to shore in a lifeboat. In this story - not too long after the romantic period when people felt a strong affinity to nature - nature loomed threateningly as a world of enormous forces hostile to life, a material world filled with brutal combat and indifference to the feeble and daunted soul of a human being. The world portrayed was one where human life could be snuffed out at any moment.

Thoughts are powerful. Thoughts like these lie behind much of modern civilization, and we are, in fact, creating such a world with alarming speed.

Shakespeare's play _The Tempest_ presents an entirely different picture. There, a shipwreck also occurs, one which causes a group of scheming men to be cast up on an island. One of them had stolen the dukedom of his brother years before and had set the brother and his daughter adrift in a leaking boat on the sea, slowly to sink and drown. The duke and his daughter were shipwrecked on this very island – they are still there. The deposed duke was an extraordinary Renaissance scholar to begin with – that was why he had, unfortunately, allowed his brother to govern his city – and during the subsequent years spent marooned on the island with his daughter, he had acquired a deep knowledge of the realm of the Nature Spirits. One in particular was beholden to him, an air spirit called Ariel.

Once the newly shipwrecked men have recovered from their own subsequent shipwreck on the island where the deposed Duke Prospero and his daughter have been living, they take up their former activities. They quarrel and they plot; two of them even plot to murder one of their own company.

Yet, all around them is another world, a world that sustains them without their knowing it. This world is described by Caliban, the most bestial human being on the island, in one of the moments when, through a window in his consciousness, the beneficence of nature flows towards him. He has been rejoicing at the coarseness and aggressiveness of the plotting castaways, but then suddenly he begins to describe to them his island. For one moment his consciousness is freed from the coarse and aggressive world he and his newfound comrades create about themselves. For a moment, he is filled with wonder and love.

> *"Be not afeared," he says to the plotters:*
> *"The isle is full of noises,*
> *Sounds and sweet airs that give delight and hurt not.*
> *Sometimes a thousand twanging instruments*
> *Will hum about mine ears, and sometimes voices*
> *That, if I had waked after long sleep,*
> *Will make me sleep again. And then, in dreaming,*
> *The clouds methought would open and show riches*
> *Ready to drop upon me, that when I waked,*
> *I cried to dream again."*

The sublime world he perceives so briefly be-tween falling asleep and waking – a world of music, won-der, and beauty – is a much greater world than the world of his feelings and intentions. It is a picture of the nature world as it once was – innocent – full of music – full of unseen beings which have been sustaining the life of the world since its beginning, beings which have helped to bring it to manifestation for ages.

Awareness of these beings lasted up until very recently. In a book on Ireland, there was a picture of a house out in the country built of great imposing stones. But surprisingly, one corner of this stone house had been sheered off from top to bottom. After it had been built, someone had discovered that a fairy road was passing through the corner of the building, so people cut off the corners of all the stones in deference to the beings streaming through. Sir Arthur Conan Doyle, who wrote the Sherlock Holmes stories, also published a collection of stories about the relationships of small children with fairies. At that time it was known that occasionally some children of a very young age would play with house fairies for awhile.

The writer of this book is an older person – over 60 years old – old enough to be aware that nature has changed drastically in the last 50 years. The rich full golden atmosphere of natural places has declined alarmingly. If the sun disappears behind a cloud, then all of a sudden one can see what has happened. It used to be that nature was busy and content within itself, full of a warm light-filled life, the life of its invisible caretakers. Now the landscape is becoming more like stage scenery – it is hardened, and sometimes it is alien and alarming.

Human beings could make a great difference. Once upon a time people would have asked for help from the spiritual world. Now, what we need to do is work! The most encouraging thing is that what we need to do is something we can do. We need to be aware of the problem, to work for practical solutions, and to become our best selves. It is not necessary to do anything magical, because the nature world can find its support today through what is evolving now out of the best in human nature. Shakespeare knew that. The darkness and storms in plays like _Macbeth_ and _King Lear_ are not fiction and fantasy: they are symptoms of times when the nature kingdoms with all their teeming beings begin to deteriorate and to become chaotic because human beings lose themselves and their sense for how to live in the best way, for the good of all.

This book is written for people who do not perceive the Nature Spirits and who might only be able to grant the possibility that in fact there might be such beings. The author grew up in the 1950s, when it was widely considered wrong to believe in anything invisible – anything at all. The irony was, that it was also a period when dozens, perhaps hundreds of science fiction stories were written, and some of those authors immediately re-invented invisible beings. A British physicist named Fred Hoyle wrote a popular novel where he invented a great disembodied consciousness formed of electricity! It is very interesting that scientifically-minded people dis-avowed with great thoroughness any knowledge of spiritual beings, but then immediately developed an interest in beings made of something like the forces they used in their machines and electronic equipment.

Any esoteric knowledge of the nature kingdoms in this book comes from the work of Rudolf Steiner. He was an Austrian philosopher and seer who lived from 1861 to 1925, and who investigated many aspects of life and the spirit.

If one knows the creation stories of many different cultures, then one knows that for ages people were aware that life comes from life. (This is true also of the book of Genesis in the Bible.) The Nature Spirits are called elemental beings. They work with the four elements: "earth" (anything solid), "water" (anything fluid), "air" (anything gaseous), and "fire" (warmth). They are the detached offspring of the angelic hierarchies, and it has been their task to bring substance (matter) into manifestation. They have been doing this for ages, and in the present time, this task presents a risk for them – the risk of losing their connection to the angelic beings, and the risk of being caught up by the material forces of the earth, those used by science and technology.

The benevolent elemental beings, according to Rudolf Steiner, are not very interested in human beings: they tend to keep away from them. They are devoted in the main to their tasks in the plant world, and the gnomes to tasks in the mineral world as well. In the plant kingdom, gnomes tend to work in the area of the roots; un-dines, who work with fluids and who can live in moisture -laden air, are active in leafing processes; sylphs (air and light) work more when plants flower; and fire spirits (salamanders) have to do with seed formation and ripening, with warmth processes.

There are many ways people can help these beings whose activity is crucial for the natural world.

> One way is through ecological solutions. Like every other being in nature, the elemental beings are experiencing habitat problems – loss of habitat, and deterioration and impoverishment of the habitat still existing.
>
> Biodynamic practices are important: they enliven the soil over time and produce a living sustainable environment which also supports the Nature Spirits.
>
> Another way is simply through who we are as people and through how we live: the way we use our senses, especially through how we see; through the quality of our memories, through what we think, feel and will to do.
>
> Our knowledge and awareness of the present state of the human being is also crucial. Do we know where we are in our evolution? Do we know what is the relationship of the human being now to what is spiritual? If we carry this knowledge in our consciousness, the beings around us will also know. For this reason, the work of a modern initiate like Rudolf Steiner can be very helpful, because the whole universe and everything in it has developed and changed. With the incarnation of the Christ, a great cosmic being, 2,000 years ago, the essential nature of the human being was brought within reach of each human being the world over – this also the nature beings need to understand.

It is important that people are aware of the situation, and that they care. Something as simple as committed caring for a place will provide a shelter for beings which are invisible.

There is much evidence that populations of wild creatures can be restored. In the 1950s, beavers were moving back into the streams of Western Massachusetts, beaver which had disappeared decades before. Now, in 2008, in a small town in central Massachusetts, bear and moose, and their young have been sighted – an unheard of experience. In Berkeley, California, on a city street surrounded by miles and miles of ordinary city, the tips of the rose bushes had all been eaten off. It was deer – a group of three deer that had come originally from the university campus, which was nonetheless quite a few blocks away. They slept in backyards behind bushes during the day and came out at night, walking up and down the streets.

There is no reason why we cannot create an environment where the less visible beings can live again; the butterflies, the bees and other insects, the birds, and even the Nature Spirits, if we are conscious of what they need in order to live. Humanity has lived in a kind of Garden of Eden for ages and ages, where everything was provided. Now, just as each person needs to know about cars and computers and other modern equipment, now we have to know how to foster and sustain all aspects of our environment. Such knowledge needs to become a matter of course.

2

ECOLOGICAL SOLUTIONS

The Importance of Flowers

The earth needs flowers! The natural environment tells us this. Even stark desert areas can be covered with flowers in spring. The magazine *Arizona Highways* made its reputation in part in the 1940s and 1950s with spectacular photographs of the desert in bloom. Death Valley in California has, at the right moment, acres of flowers. In Craters of the Moon National Monument in Idaho, which is almost nothing but miles of broken basaltic lava, the few conical hills of basaltic sand, after a rain, are covered with tiny flowers one can scarcely see – some no more than $1/8^{th}$ or $1/4^{th}$ of an inch high. In mountains there are sub-alpine flowers hugging the ground where the snow scarcely melts, and at the shore hardy well-protected plants living in the midst, almost buried, of miles of sand dunes. High in the Oregon Cascades when the snow packs disappear in early summer, there, poking up at the borders of the last thin crust of snow are carpets and carpets of flowers. And so it is throughout the dense forests: carpets of flowers before the deciduous trees have leafed out, shrubs and berry canes or bushes which blossom later, and flowering trees. In Massachusetts, after a six months' winter, the woods once were full of Mayflowers, and then Polyganum, and sometimes lady slippers; and Mountain laurel, shadbush, and wild cherry trees. The sheer cliff faces towering above the glacier-fed streams rushing into the Columbia River for a short time in spring are covered with ferns, shooting stars, penstamen, yellow monkey flowers, and red paint brush, all growing in the crevices. Flowers are an extremely significant part of the life cycle of the Earth.

It seems that on some level, people know how important they are. The last twenty to thirty years, there have been significant flower projects in various places in the country. In several East Coast states, the median strips of major highways, for long distances, were plowed and then seeded with wild flower mixtures. In Portland, Oregon, on the other side of the country, a woman convinced the city to plant wild flower mixtures along the roads and in the intersections in many parts of the city. Currently, dozens of rose bushes have been planted along highway interchanges at the borders of downtown. It is normal for banks, supermarkets, and other businesses to plant flowering trees around the parking lots and once in a while, apple or pear trees. In some older neighbor-hoods, the long streets are lined with old Norway maples – golden avenues in spring because of the flowers, golden avenues in fall because of the leaves.

There are possibilities everywhere. Along High-way 99E South of Albany, Oregon, the Camas flowers which once formed virtual lakes of blooms where the farms now are, the flowers still bloom in the ditches, and people have planted daffodils which line the highway for miles. Highways in Los Angeles are hemmed in by banks matted with wild flowers in many colors, and often Oleander bushes in red and white. In a small quiet town in the hills in central Massachusetts, a Dunkin' Donuts shop has filled the entire area in front with red, yellow, orange, and purple flowers.

People in other countries also have a love for flowers: one thinks of the flower boxes outside the windows of houses in Normandy, France and many other places; the meticulously cared for flower plots in traffic circles and around monuments; and the acres of garden plots outside European cities, some with tiny houses on one end so that a garden plot can become like a vacation home. In Dornach and Arlesheim, towns near Basle, Switzerland, for several months the lawns are full of successions of flowers; first snow drops and tiny yellow anemones, then crocuses of light lavender with bright yellow-orange stamens, and finally self-sowing primroses of many colors – hundreds and perhaps thousands of flowers per house. Throughout the spring, those parts of the lawn are never mown until May 1, when the flowers have all gone by. From March to May, the grass grows ragged, and no one minds. If a mower comes, he mows around the flowers and leaves pools of meadowland in the middle of the lawn.

We could change our minds about golf course lawns. We could sow our lawns with white clover, which the bees love. There is also a small yellow medic, a leguminous plant with inconspicuous yellow flowers, which grows flat against the ground and slips under the grass clumps in the lawn. It almost can't be seen, but it gives nitrogen to the soil and produces flowers for a long time. Empty lots could be tilled and seeded with vetch, which bees also love.

Why is this important as we consider the plight of the Nature Spirits?

The carpets of flowers are actually a crucial part of the invisible cycle of the Earth's life. The tendency simply to annihilate whole areas of soil and cover them with asphalt is very prevalent; to spread flame retardants through the wilderness forests in fire season, or herbicides in logged over areas or along roads. Once upon a time the Eastern forests were sprayed from the air year after year with DDT to kill the Gypsy moth. In the suburbs, companies come in and mist whole yards with poisons to get rid of everything but the grass, fine mists which drift onto neighboring properties; combination lawn fertilizers laced with herbicides are a given. And we are permeating absolutely everything with artificial forces and machine vibrations, cell phone towers being one of the most recent sources. The fields from computer equipment can fill whole houses (a young man said a big screen TV set did that in his home). Do these force-fields leak out? It would be important to know.

Nature Spirits are the true chemists of the world. All of this is alien to them, and a hindrance to all of nature.

Spiritually, the Earth is itself a living being, but it doesn't have eyes as we do. Spiritually, the plant world is not separate from the Earth. The plant world is the organ of perception of the earth, as well as its organs of digestion in a certain sense. The plants look up at the heavenly world, from where the activity of creation originally came. In early spring, a tremendous surge of activity occurs in the plant kingdom: first, a great spurt of root growth which, of course, we can't see, and then the surprisingly prolific sprouting and leafing. According to Rudolf Steiner all of this occurs because of previous cosmic influences and especially because of the stored up forces of last year's sun, stored beneath the ground, often at considerable depth. The wonderful sprouting and leafing which one sees everywhere is actually the result of forces and influences given over to the Earth the previous year. (Most of what is included here comes from Rudolf Steiner's lecture course *Man as Symphony of the Creative Word*, one of his most difficult esoteric works.) When the flowers appear, however, then the present influences of the cosmos have become active in very complex and often indirect ways through processes taking place within the sphere of life. The Earth, Rudolf Steiner said, perceives its cosmic environment through what happens in the plants, especially during the flower and seed formation stages. The Earth perceives it, at least in part, when plant remains fall upon the earth and gradually become part of it.

Because of this, rotting is a time of rejoicing! Elemental beings, the Nature Spirits, come to the surface of the Earth and bring back down into it what is given over to it by the plants. These beings are also positively jubilant when, in a pasture of grazing cattle, manure falls upon the ground. The manure is permeated both by what the cow took in as it grazed and also by its own nature. This is why the cow was a sacred animal in so many places. The Nature Spirits are very active in connection with these processes.

The elemental beings traditionally known as gnomes, those who work with the solid aspects of the world, actually do not see the solid earth. It is like a space to them, where different concentrations of minerals seem to them like different atmospheres as they wander within the Earth. They don't like it; they feel as if they are imprisoned; they long for the pictures of the cosmos which rain down to them because of the plants. They are intensely interested in what descends from the rotting plants down into the earth. They keep it and care for it over the winter and carry it from place to place as they wander within the Earth.

For some decades now, human beings have been substituting "mineral" processes for natural ones through the use of inorganic fertilizers, where what is brought to the plants is a dead chemical substance. What brings the plants into manifestation is thrown out of balance, and the deadening effect on plants is quite obvious. Even though the plants may be greener – a deep heavy dark green –

they are deader, and full of material substance. Flavor and overall quality of fruits and vegetables grown in this way usually deteriorates in spite of their large size. It is very likely that such plants no longer carry into the Earth what it needs. Areas where plants are allowed to grow organically and where flowering plants are encouraged, these provide something for the whole earth, and for the invisible beings which work there.

The second class of elemental beings, the undines, work with what is liquid. Like the other elemental beings, they prefer to live at the interfaces between elements – for example, where small streams dash over rocks, splashing and foaming, where air and water, plant life and solid rocks are all there together. Such places are "alive". The undines work in the moist air around the plant leaves, also in bodies of water, including oceans. Sometimes in paintings and in older photographs it is possible to see how much gentler the landscape is where undines are prevalent. The photographer Samuel Chamberlain, who took many photographs of New England and even France in the mid-twentieth century, managed to capture something of this aspect in his landscape photographs. Now in these times, it can be necessary to create such an environment through proper planning.

A biodynamic farm in a starkly dry area of New Mexico had to create its own microclimate by placing their garden right behind or alongside buildings where it would be protected from the strong desert winds. The farmers built low walls around the gardens, planted hedges, and mulched the soil so that the plants would be able to create a microclimate within the garden in that severe world of rock and sky and wind. It is possible, of course, that an environment can become too dark, too moist, and too full of rankly growing vegetation. Then, it may be necessary to do some pruning or even to take out bushes and trees.

Both the choice of appropriate plants and the overall planning in creating a landscape environment can go a long way towards providing a welcome habitat for the Nature Spirits. A certain amount of considerate awareness is also important. If plants have to be weeded out, it is a good idea to warn the Nature Spirits ahead of time, perhaps two or three days. It is particularly distressing to them if whole areas of plants are pulled out when they are flowering – planning ahead helps a great deal. It also causes pain to the earth if plants are simply pulled out of the ground when they are tightly rooted to it. In that case, one can loosen the soil first with a spading fork.

We are living in a time when it is important to develop a new consciousness and a more advanced conception of care-taking. Whenever people can spend time helping to foster healthy gardens, lawns, woodlots, fields, or even larger landscapes, it will help. There is always the possibility that children in the family, or retired people may be quite gifted and full of insights for what could be done. A twelve-year-old boy once accompanied his father, who was showing a group of farmers and property owners how to thin and prune a woodlot. Midway through the workshop the boy took over and began to talk and demonstrate. He could have done the whole workshop! It was very inspiring: he was able to let in air and light by making cuts so skillfully and with such good judgment that, once it had been done, you didn't know anything had changed. The woods seemed quite simply "more themselves."

The landscape is becoming impoverished. Attentiveness to the need for flowers, as many as possible, whether in the corner of a yard or in a Nature Conservancy project involving acres of wilderness, is very important. However, there is more: the bird, bee, insect and butterfly populations. These are of crucial importance spiritually, in a spiritual ecological sense, because if those populations disappear, the life goes out of the landscape even if it is full of flowers.

The air spirits (the sylphs) store up light within the atmosphere the way the gnomes take care of forces from the sun and cosmos within the Earth. The air and fire spirits need the birds and the insects. The plants have a kind of consciousness – a sunny asleep consciousness. But the insect, bird, and animal worlds have something more: they perceive, they are aware, they are active, they feel. They have what is called an astral nature, something of the nature of soul, and if this is missing from the landscape environment, the plant and nature spirit kingdoms are quite simply bereft.

Insects and Birds

More than the flowers, the world of insects, butterflies, and birds in urban or almost-urban environments has suffered immensely. Places with many gardens and streets lined with flowering trees now have very few birds compared with 30 years ago. The butterflies are even more rare.

Spiritually, this is a tragedy for the earth, and for the spiritual universe as well. One aspect of what Rudolf Steiner was able to bring to humanity through his research was a spiritual ecological knowledge, because what seem to be very humble creatures of nature which we scarcely notice have important roles to play. The butterflies, for example, can do what no other creatures can do: they spiritualize substance while they live. There is a "rain" of light, of substance spiritualized into light, ascending upwards from the Earth from the butterflies. The birds do this also, but they release this light spiritualized from substance only when they die. So, it is a tragedy on a large scale when butterflies and birds decline, and when the habitat which supports them is neglected or destroyed.

A teenager named James Alexander lived in southern Oregon. As a child, he and his family raised butterfly and moth caterpillars; they watched them build their cocoons and then saw the butterflies and moths emerge, spectacular ones which they bought from butterfly breeders. Butterflies meant so much to him, that by the time he was 16, all he wanted for Christmas (or perhaps it was his birthday) was a huge professional encyclopedic volume describing different butterfly species. The decline of the monarch butterfly population worried him, so he flew with his mother to the East Coast to collect milkweed seeds to sow along the roadsides near his home – forage for the butterflies. By the time he was 17, he was giving talks on butterflies to adult groups and working with people to set up a butterfly reserve in the Siskiyou Wilderness area. He put together seed packets of host plants for butterflies and sold dry flower arrangements with chrysalises in them at the Ashland Saturday market so that people could hatch and release the butterflies at home.

Lack of awareness of the life cycles of all these creatures can have devastating consequences of which modern humanity is almost completely unaware. A college bought an extra lot which bordered on its own land. A very tall dense long hedge of English holly, where homeless men hid, drinking, divided the two properties from one another. The college decided to cut it down – in May.

The hedge was full of nesting birds. There were community gardens on the neighboring college property, and it was a joy to be there on an afternoon or early evening in spring or early summer. The swallows wheeled and soared through the sky, weaving and looping over the fields and gardens. But when the chain saws had felled the hedge, which was perhaps a half of a block long, hundreds of birds swarmed and swirled in the sky over the place where the hedge had been, crying and crying, for at least three days. For people who knew what had happened, it was a terrible sight.

By way of contrast in 1990 the city newspapers in Portland, Oregon ran more than one story about a man and Sauvie Island – a large flat diked island with farms and woods out in the middle of the Columbia River. This man, David Fouts was a respiratory therapist at the veterans' hospital, and he loved purple martins, which were disappearing. As a child in Chicago, his family had kept apartment houses for purple martins in the backyard, and he loved their song. So, he began building Martin apartment houses to bring back the martins to Sauvie Island. He did research on the use of hollow gourds which Indians had used in the South to encourage martin populations to settle near them, long before the Europeans came. Slaves in the American South had learned from the Indians, and they too made gourd-house-communities for the martins.

When David Fouts began setting up houses for martins on Sauvie Island, there were only 20 pairs of martins. Five years later, on one tip of the island, there were 80 pairs. He had learned to build houses that martins would accept and which discouraged starlings. Starlings like to nest in the dark, so he painted the interiors of the gourds white and cut a small window across the back. He found that if he hung the gourds on a line, they would swing in the wind. The martins would live there, content, but the swinging would discourage other birds.

Another story: At Chapman Elementary School in Northwest Portland, years ago, someone noticed in late summer and early fall that Vaux's Swifts were diving into the large steam vent chimney at dusk where they would rest, clinging to the inside of the chimney. In early September, they came by the hundreds and then thousands as they migrated through the area. For a number of years, the school didn't turn the heating system on in the fall until the birds had left. But finally, the school had a crucial decision to make: should they cap the chimney to keep the birds out? They decided: no. They gave the chimney to the birds.

Now, in the early evening in September, whole families flock to the school – children, people in wheelchairs, people with walkers, people of many nationalities. They sit on the lawn for about 1 1/2 hours before dusk and wait, perhaps eating picnic suppers. As the sun goes down, the birds approach, just a few at first, dark forms a little like swallows, rocketing across the sky, swooping down toward the chimney and pulling out of their dive just short of it. Then, they sweep off into nothingness, or they join the vortex of birds swirling high above the chimney. An occasional bird breaks out of the vortex, dives down toward the chimney, and then rockets back up to join the others, weaving and swirling. Then, when the sun sinks behind the West Hills which border the Willamette River which joins the Columbia at the Washington border close by, then the whole swirling mass of birds dissolves and they fly away north toward the Columbia, leaving a silent and deepening blue sky.

The crowd grows silent – the school lawn is crowded. People walk up the sidewalks from the neighborhood to look – there are no parking places anywhere. Ten minutes. Fifteen minutes. Nothing. People sit still. Suddenly, black dots appear high in the sky. A bird emerges from the darkening blue, plummets down toward the tower, turns around just above it, and flutters down backwards into the chimney. Hundreds come, thousands, then tens of thousands, all into one chimney for the night. How warm and alive it must be inside! The birds return for about a month.

The sylphs, the class of Nature Spirits which weave the effects of light into the plants, love the birds. The fire spirits which become especially active as the flower pollen is scattered and as fruit ripens, love the bees. They follow insects. Rudolf Steiner said that a seer can perceive the sylphs as a light aura around the birds, and the fire spirits as an aura around the bees. These spirits follow the bees and the birds so closely that it is difficult to distinguish them. The sylphs following swallows or seagulls live in the music which streams out of the flight path of the soaring bird. If the insects, butterflies, and birds disappear, then for the Nature Spirits, it would be as if a young child suddenly lost a parent or his family.

This may be why, when there are almost no butterflies, few bees, and very few birds, a place can seem full of stage scenery – it loses its atmosphere and it can seem utterly material, just the way we have been taught to think it is. Normally, the sylphs would help to store light and to hold it in reserve in the air, the fire spirits would hold the warmth. But something has happened: the invisible beings which help to create a sun-lit atmosphere in a place aren't there, at least not enough of them.

Habitat Restoration

It is probably clear by now that an enormous amount can be accomplished even by people who have no awareness of the Nature Spirits. An enormous amount can be done by people who simply love nature, who want to care for it, and who are interested in some aspect of it.

People often wonder: do we need to do something magical? But many of the most severe problems facing the Nature Spirits are habitat problems: they are ecological. These beings simply need to have places to live and work, and they need the bees, butterflies, beneficial insects and birds, who are also experiencing habitat problems. In the British Isles, for example, there is a centuries' old practice of creating hedgerows which separate fields and line the roads, hedgerows which bloom, which have berries, and provide shelter for birds, insects, and other creatures. (See the <u>National Geographic</u> issue of September, 1993. With luck, one can find one at a recycling center.) It is important for us to develop our own practices.

Borders of some kind help to define the area one is caring for. Farms in southern France, for example, are often sheltered from severe seasonal winds by a closely planted row of tall thin-spired cypress trees. In the American West it was often rows of Cottonwood trees. Each place will begin to have an atmosphere of its own -- to be a kind of oasis. The more the benevolent spirits come to work there, the more that will be true.

The humanizing influence is also important. The fact that a person is there working upon a property or natural area can have quite an effect. Someone goes out into a yard or walks the fields on a farm and thinks: what should be done here? What would be good? In a yard, he may decide to site a vegetable or flower garden in one part of it, with possibly a border of raspberry canes along one side and an herb garden along another, with a circle of chairs under a tree for people to sit and enjoy in the garden, and converse. Or he may build rock terraces or rivers of pebbles, or a small pool in the shade of a bush. Season after season, many days, he or she goes out and looks – is glad to see a robin or a warbler, or a butterfly which hasn't come for a long time. The person decides it would be possible to plant a small tree somewhere, or ground cover under the bushes. As the weather changes, he becomes aware of the effects. And sometimes children come to play.

It is the care-taking and the appreciation which matter, the constant awareness and involvement. If in one corner of his or her mind, the person knows that the plants are flourishing because of the Nature Spirits and because of the presence of so much diversity of life, if he knows that everything would become more disconnected, more "thing-like" and material if the Nature Spirits weren't there, then his awareness will create a spiritual environment for the invisible care-takers where they can live, and they will begin to "follow", and to help what is being done; their work will complement the work of the human being.

Things have reached a state, however, where it will not be easy to maintain a good environment – it will take a lot of initiative and determination. But, all over, many people who have always had a strong interest in the natural world are ready to work very hard to sustain what is already there and to create new natural environments.

Each area will have its own sources of information. Often an organization like the Audubon Society, the Nature Conservancy, a local Native Plant or Hardy Plant Society, or specialized plant nurseries can give advice on finding good local contacts. Several people have mentioned The Xerces Society, which is dedicated to preserving different types of insects, and said that it also has people who have a lot of valuable information about other things as well.

The following organizations and businesses in the vicinity of Portland, Oregon are samples of what one might find in one's own area.

The Xerces Society for Invertebrate Conservation,
Portland, Oregon: 503-232-6639
They have a number of excellent information sheets on conserving native bees, but

terflies, and insects, and lists of forage plants, some by region.

The Portland Nursery: 503-231-5050/ 503-788-9000
They have a substantial lists of forage plants for butterflies, hummingbirds, and birds, also a list of cover crops. Their garden information corner is always staffed, and they have important reference works close at hand.

The Backyard Bird Shop: 503-496-0908
There are several in the city. These shops stock birdbaths, water features, all kinds of birdhouses and feeders, and bird food – almost anything any one could want. The staff are very knowledgeable and have a lot of practical information and experience. Booklets are available, also very useful handouts on bird houses and feeders.

The Audubon Society, Portland: 503-292-9453
They have a store, books, handouts, and people who can answer questions.

Bosky Dell Natives, West Linn,Oregon: 503-638-5945
A large selection of native plants, many of which will grow in the shade, including berry-bearing trees and shrubs.

One Green World, Molalla, Oregon: 877-353-4028
A wonderful color catalog worth having just for itself, full of shrubs and trees with edible fruits and berries from Europe, Asia, Africa, North America – all over the world. Excellent. Mind expanding! www.onegreenworld.com.

Sometimes community colleges, parks, or formal gardens will have knowledgeable people who teach courses and host events (like a Horticultural Society meeting, for example), where it is possible to make contact with people who know what is available in one's own area.

Many people sense that the natural environment is in trouble, even in what appear to be well-kept neighborhoods or wild areas. A city which is absolutely full of flowers for months is often losing its insects and birds. Bosky Dell, the native plant nursery near Portland, Oregon, has birdhouses everywhere and a fenced-in pool surrounded by native bushes and plants. It is crowded with all kinds of birds, singing and flitting from tree to tree. It might be possible, for example, in an urban or suburban neighborhood for several families to get together to create such an environment, or to have sufficient plantings in the neighborhood for butterflies or bees to last throughout the season, or an array of different berries and seeds for birds. People would need to research what kinds of flowers truly can sustain a bee population – sowing white clover into the lawns instead of eradicating it would definitely help! It would be particularly important to find out what kinds of flowers would be good bee forage in September, when most of the flowers are gone.

It will take time for the birds and insects to come back, perhaps even longer for the butterflies. But our environment will be poorer and more material, even in the wilderness areas, the more we simply let it be, let it slide, while everything that can contribute to a rich complex natural system wanes, or leaves.

In the 1970s, in the beginning of the environmental movement in Portland, three groups of women, unknown to one another, started up spontaneously and independently of one another in three distant corners of the city: in the southwest, the northeast and southeast.

Each group met regularly, gathered information on recycling and ways of avoiding creating pollution and on urgent local problems. They then lent out two or three volunteer speakers at a time. Other people would invite friends or colleagues to morning coffees, evening dessert gatherings, or to potlucks, and the three women's groups would supply speakers (usually at least two) and handouts on environmental problems and on what people could do.

These gatherings were very successful. Eventually, the three groups discovered one another! Within a year they were taking on bigger, tougher problems and were speaking before the City Council, the Planning Commission, governmental environmental agencies, and the state legislature. Their efforts had a lasting effect on city government. Much of what needs to be done to address the environmental crisis which impacts the Nature Spirits could be taken up by neighborhood groups, by businesses, school classes, boy scouts and girl scouts, summer camps, and groups of friends, simply out of an interest in restoring the natural environment or in creating a new one.

We are at a turning point in our cultural history. We have come to the point where we need to completely redo our culture: we need to create the kind of environment the world needs instead of simply participating in what is already there.

We already have much of the knowledge and experience we need. If such an outlook and commitment becomes more central to our culture, then, as a side effect, it will benefit young people greatly, especially if they work alongside the adults, take part in the potlucks and bee or bird-fests, do some of the research, and even lead, as many of them are capable of doing. People will forge new relationships, and a deep sense of community will arise – something much more extensive than the work-place community to which people have become accustomed.

The invisible community, the four classes of Nature Spirits, will be aware of everything we do and why we do it, and they will work along with us instead of withdrawing, even though we don't see them. This is a much larger issue than simply creating attractive natural landscapes; it has to do with creating a living environment where something much warmer and finer can come about than the material world which is appearing by default.

It will matter to the Nature Spirits that we know they are there and that we know and are grateful for what they do. It may be, that if people have simply read this book, that will help a great deal. Just as a child knows what is going on between adults even if they don't say anything, other beings also know. What happens in the future will depend to a large extent upon the degree to which people care.

The Human Presence

Human beings are very important to nature. According to Rudolf Steiner, if human beings were suddenly to disappear, nature itself would degenerate and deteriorate. When Daniel Boone and the other explorers first crossed the Appalachian Mountains from the original Thirteen Colonies and entered into the trackless "West", they found vast forests with immense trees and great glades, on and on, for miles. Onward the explorers walked in amazement and wonder. Hints of these forests can be seen in an occasional painting from the 1800s. The Native Americans had been setting low, slow-burning fires in the forests for centuries, clearing the brush so that they could walk and hunt there. The bigger trees survived the fires and grew into a magnificent canopy.

Today, forests are often full of thickets and brush. Twenty years ago, an old logger, a man in his 70s, told me that in his childhood, the forests where he lived on the Oregon Coast were clear! No one believes it, he said. You could walk in the forest. Now, it would be impossible to go even 20 feet – the forest floor is covered with rotting fallen giants, choked with new trees and saplings of various sizes growing out of the decaying trunks and tall dense masses of salal and other shrubs. The Native Americans, he said, were also keeping the coastal forests clear with their fires.

The Native Americans, more than many other peoples, lived with a profound gratitude for what met them in nature. Such gratitude contributes to the spiritual environment of a place.

Simple awareness and appreciation can be very sustaining for the world of the Nature Spirits. A photographer, Marcia Keegan, published a book called _Mother Earth, Father Sky_ with pictures of the American Southwest, accompanied by Native American chants. There is a wonderful picture of a Native American woman with a basket, tossing a heap of corn kernels into the air to winnow out the chaff and catching them in the basket. "Rise up, rise up," says the chant, "my yellow corn maidens, and I will sing for you!"

In the romantic paintings of the mid-1800s, appreciation for nature is very evident. Sometimes it is almost possible to perceive the elemental beings, at least to see the quality of their effect upon the landscape: the gnarled tough appearance of tree trunks, snags, and rock ledges which manifest something of the nature of the gnomes; the misty quality of the moisture-laden air which signals the presence of the undines, and the shining radiance in

Joseph William Turner's paintings which hints at an ocean of sylphs at the visible edge of any source of light.

About 20 years ago there was an old man, a rigorous even aggressive person who was an exceptional classical pianist, the best in the Northwest, people said. He was also a collector of fine furniture and of art works, and he mainly lived off his inheritance. He accepted only a partial salary and otherwise taught his students out of pure commitment and love. But he was difficult – very critical – and not everyone could live near him. For many, he was one of the most important people in their lives, and for some, a real trial.

His backyard, however, was extraordinary. There wasn't much in it – it was surrounded by a hedge; the lawn was thick, but it was a live green, not a deadened heavy over-fertilized green. Just inside the hedge and against the house were a few bushes, well-kept, some of them probably rhododendrons. Yet, even though there was not much there, the yard was as if filled with sunlight, a sunlight which belonged to the yard itself. It seemed to be full of elementals, beneficent elementals. His house, inside, was much the same. (There are also house fairies.) In the house there was also a definite constructive, warm-lit atmosphere. This was a shock. How could a person who could be so loudly angry have attracted so many constructive invisible beings?

He was an unusual man, even a great man, a person of strong love for things, for creatures of the nature world, of strong love for human beings, a love which went far beyond what people are usually capable of. Everything was well cared for. Everything he ever bought meant something to him, and he appreciated it. To see him look at a duck (which he considered to be a particularly kind and welcome member of the bird kingdom) was a lesson in seeing.

One day he was waiting for a former student, whom he loved as he did just about all of them. He was a master at perceiving, recognizing, and understanding the value of individual differences in people. The student was young and unreliable and might come very late, or even not at all, and the man knew that, and yet, he had prepared the house to welcome him. It was almost evening, and the light bulbs in the lamps had been chosen so that the light was neither too bright nor too dim – it was welcoming. Everything was thought through, felt through, carefully decided upon. And the house and yard seemed absolutely packed with invisible beings who wanted to live there. Manfred Schmidt-Brabant, previously President of the Anthroposophical Society founded by Rudolf Steiner, said that now in modern times it will be important to arrive at a sacramental way of living in our daily life – not necessarily through traditional ritual, but out of a sense for how to live devotedly in everything we do. This was a man who wanted to do that – in his own unique way.

An old retired person, even someone almost disabled, and especially an older person who lives alone – an older person will often care for a house or a garden in a completely quiet, devoted, and committed way. Modern life doesn't tug at them and disorient them. In New England, perhaps two decades ago, there seemed to be an unusual number of older people living alone, doing whatever tasks they had to do out of interest, and out of a commitment to do the work as it needs to be done. If a small child can experience this, be it a grandparent or simply a person who lives nearby, it will be of great benefit to the child. And one always has the sense that the Nature Spirits and the elemental beings in the house or garden are working in a quiet orderly way as well, that there is happiness there.

Even our industrial corporate world could be different from the way it usually is: for example, the ING Building in Amsterdam, Holland. It is an international corporate bank headquarters, constructed from 1983-1986. The man who was instrumental in determining what it became was an officer of the bank, a President or Vice-President, who was familiar with Rudolf Steiner's work. When it came time to build a new corporate headquarters, he surveyed all the people in the bank, including all the employees, and asked them what they needed. As plans developed and as construction proceeded, he went back to them over and over again, so that all the people were able to make continuing contributions to this revolutionary building.

The building consists of 10 pentagonal towers constructed so that the hot air will rise up and fresh air will come in. Much of the problem of heating the building in winter and cooling it in summer is taken care of by the unusual design. People wanted natural light, so there are great windows everywhere, some with stained glass window sections: warm colors (red, orange, yellow) on the north side of the building, and cool colors (greens, blues, violet) on the south. Offices have windows which open. All over the building, the lighting is in large part natural, and where electric lights are necessary, they are so artistically designed and placed that they cast light in a way which is healing. In the corners, they seem to glow. The walkways which pass from tower to tower are lined with art works. There are water features throughout the building, for example, a large flat pool beneath a stairwell across from an elevator, and behind it a glass wall with artistic natural-looking designs engraved into it. Water drips quietly into the pool. It is a healing building.

They also wanted a building which welcomed the natural world. On the south side, where, beyond the building, the traffic churns by constantly, is a narrow "forest" of twenty-year-old trees shading the windows from the hot sun in summer. A path threads through it, a good place to take a walk, where one would scarcely be aware of the endless blocks of traffic and cement and buildings beyond. On the forest side of the building is also a Japanese garden in a deep pit – like an orchestra pit – with a large pool at the bottom. A small stream cascades into the pool. People can go there and chat or eat their lunches in the sun by the pool with the splashing water, bushes, and water plants. On the other side of the building one or two stories up, next to the main restaurant and several meeting rooms, is the Finnish garden – a roof -top garden filled with flowers, bushes, archways over the paths covered with leafing and flowering vines, and large banks of culinary herbs for the restaurant. People wander alone or talking to friends on the sunlit paths through the garden, which is quite extensive. Where the paths widen out, there are benches in bower-like places where people can sit for a private conversation. Over near the wall, water wells up through crevices in between the stones in the walkway, crevices filled with small water plants, and it trickles toward a great water basin below as large as a sizeable hall. More water cascades in a rush down into the basin from a Flowform, which sends the water dashing and spiraling back and forth, finally to plunge into the great pool below. The rushing water in the form splashes in the rhythm of a steady heartbeat: the sound is very calming, refreshing, and healing. Inside the building, water trickles down a Flowform built into the railing of the main staircase, like an opera-house staircase, and splashes down into a small fountain at the end. In the towers, which have banks of window rising up to the top, green vines cascade down many floors.

After the building was completed, the employee absentee rate dropped 25%. No wonder! A visitor almost doesn't want to go home. They experienced much less illness, and, overall, lower blood pressure rates. Eighty percent of the heating, cooling, and electrical capacity is provided by the building itself. It saves several million dollars each year in fuel bills, and after it was constructed, it achieved far and away the lowest rate of energy consumption in the world. Bees populate the roof-top garden, and "the forest" on the other side and the Japanese garden have many birds. The atmosphere of this building is indescribable: it can feel more healing than the natural world. It was actually cost-effective to build because of all the savings.

Any project like this benefits the whole world, and not just the human world. It doesn't matter if the project is a wilderness sanctuary, a restoration of acres of prairie, a farm, a backyard, or a corporation campus. The spirit of the people who fostered or created anything like this and the soul/spirit relationship of the people who maintain it, are nourishment for all the invisible life of the earth. We have not yet really begun to use the creativity we have, nor our capacity to work for the betterment of the world and of human beings, whether in an urban setting, or in a suburban environment, in rural areas, or where there is wilderness. If all the people who feel called to such activity could find a place to do it, it would be a tremendous help as the world struggles with greater incidences of over-population, pollution, and stress. We still have time, but perhaps not a lot!

3

THE SIGNIFICANCE OF BIOYNAMIC PRINCIPLES FOR THE NATURE KINGDOM

For over eighty years now, people in many parts of the world have been growing food biodynamically. The method originated in Germany from a course which Rudolf Steiner gave to a group of farmers in Koberwitz in 1924.

The food is more balanced and more complex than organic or wild food. Often people who have been weakened for some reason – recovery from an operation or a debilitating condition or long periods of stress – know instantly that there is something different about it: it is more revitalizing and sustaining.

Biodynamically treated property is a refuge for Nature Spirits – they are attracted to it. Originally, the landscape the Native Americans knew was more alive, more beneficent in spirit than it is now. Through biodynamic practices, it is possible to restore some of the living quality of the land, and it becomes much kinder.

The farmers at Rudolf Steiner's course of lectures in 1924 approached him with a whole array of questions: why were their seed strains degenerating? Why couldn't they grow the same food in the same field for as many years as they had previously? Why were their animals sometimes sterile and why did more of them have diseases?

The problem, Rudolf Steiner said, originates in the soil. The vitality of the soil had declined. With biodynamic treatment the land and plant-life are restored to their normal condition: they are no longer "stage-scenery", the remote and alien state which is appearing in the natural world more and more.

A normal plant has a gracious appearance. If plants are grown with ordinary chemical fertilizers, they are often a deep, heavy, dead green, rankly growing. The leaves and fruits may be very large, even swollen and distorted, and internally, they will likely be full of too much water and unfinished substance, which can often deteriorate quickly. Biodynamic produce, on the other hand, has been known for many years for its flavor and keeping quality. All of the negative symptoms described above indicate that the processes of developing life in the plant are not proceeding in the right way, which means that something has also gone wrong in the kingdom of Nature Spirits: they aren't able to work with the plants as they should. What people are doing from the material side of life is disrupting the way they need to work. A sketch follows of some of the main aspects of the biodynamic method, which is based upon composting and the use of several spray preparations.

The Compost Pile

First one makes a compost pile and inserts into it five of the six biodynamic compost preparations: the yarrow, chamomile, oak bark, stinging nettle, and dandelion preparations. Each of these plants goes through the manifestation process of a plant in an optimal way. Through the preparation-making process, each becomes a small, homeopathic compost inoculant. (Most of the preparations are flowers.) Then the sixth preparation, fermented Valerian juice, is diluted in water, stirred, and sprinkled all over the pile. The compost pile needs at least three months to ripen and possibly longer, depending upon moisture, warmth, and climate.

The Spray Preparations 500 and 501

There are two life-enhancing spray preparations. Both have to be stirred in a pail of water for an hour without stopping before spraying them out. Preparation 500 (horn manure) should be sprinkled (rain drop size) or sprayed on bare ground in the afternoon. In hot climates, it might be necessary to do the stirring and spraying in the evening. Preparation 501 (horn silica – quartz dust) is sprayed on foliage, including grass, in the morning before noon. (Rudolf Steiner warned that there are cosmic forces coming in approximately noon to 2 p.m. which should not pass into food for human consumption: so one doesn't do anything between noon and about 2:30 p.m. An experience: Once, up in a meadow of wild flowers on a mountain, the bees all disappeared shortly before noon and only reappeared on the flowers about 2:45 p.m.!)

The compost and spray preparations all strengthen the nature processes; even the ground quartz preparation does so. Plants are already surrounded in a certain way by homeopathic silica dissolved in water – it is found in part in the fine hairs on the leaves or stems and in the waxes on the leaves. The dissolved silica helps them to utilize light. (In the West the role of silica is not known, but in Japan, if the rice stems are deficient in silica, there is a danger the rice will "lodge"; it will fall over into the water in the rice paddies instead of standing upright.)

The Stirring of the Preparations

Any preparation where stirring is required should be stirred continuously without stopping for the recommended amount of time.

Advance preparation is often important. Chlorinated tap water should sit out 2-3 days in a glass container to let the chlorine evaporate out. Before starting the stirring there are several things which may need to be checked. If you will be sitting on a stool, is the ground firm? Or will one leg sink down into it? What about the sun? In half an hour will it be too hot, or shining in your eyes? And what about allergies?

It is a good idea to have several stirring sticks of different lengths and widths and to try them out in plain water before starting, because, over the course of an hour, an eighth of an inch difference in thickness can make the task either easier or considerably harder. The pail should be made of an inert substance (not metal), wood or used plastic. With smaller quantities of water – for example, for the valerian preparation – a large peanut butter jar would be sufficient.

After adding the preparation to the water in the pail, stir strongly around the pail until a vortex forms in one direction. After holding it a few seconds, then reverse direction abruptly and stir until a vortex forms in the other direction, and so on for the amount of time required. When you reverse and begin stirring in the opposite direction, a foaming chaos will occur. The churning chaos is important. This is what a rapidly dashing mountain stream does!

The two spray preparations are, in a way, opposites. The quartz Preparation 501 is a very significant one: it has a definitive effect on the development of vitamins, sugars, and flavor, as well as other things. Preparation 501 is sprayed on foliage (anything green) in the morning as early as one can manage. The morning is the daily out-breathing period of the Earth, when seeds tend to sprout and plants grow up and outward. (A caution: don't spray new transplants with 501: the plants need to develop a good root system first.)

Cow manure is the basis of Preparation 500 – the horn manure preparation. Rudolf Steiner described the elemental beings leaping and rejoicing in pastures as the cows grazed there and gave over their manure to the Earth! Preparation 500 is sprayed on bare ground in the afternoon or early evening during the in-breathing time, when things tend to work downward. (This is also a better time to prune or to do transplants.) One can sprinkle preparation 500 by hand or with a sheaf of grass, a bunch of thin twigs, or a whiskbroom dipped into the stirred preparation. For 501, a plastic spray bottle is adequate for treating small areas; for larger areas, one needs spraying equipment with a nozzle which will produce a fine mist for larger areas.

Details of Building a Compost Pile

It is important for the pile to be in contact with the bare earth. It can be set in a shallow pit 8" to 12" deep. Hopefully, there will be some cow manure in it, even if it is necessary to bring home several buckets of cow pies from a farm in the country. Horse, sheep, goat, llama, chicken, or rabbit manures are good also, but they don't quite achieve the good effect of cow manure, although horse manure comes fairly close. There is a reason why the cow was a sacred animal in many cultures! On a farm, the pile would probably be composed mainly of manure with bedding in it, run through a manure spreader to make windrow piles approximately 8' wide and 2 1/2 – 3' high. A backyard pile will usually be composed of lawn clippings, leaves, collected weeds, kitchen refuse and whatever manure one can obtain. Some things should not be put in the pile. For example, meat should be avoided, because it will attract rats. Also, morning glory, ivy, and grass roots will only multiply and cause trouble. Nut tree leaves may be too acid, but it's always possible to try them out and see if they will decompose well.

The pile will decompose most readily if the layers are no more than 2" to 3" thick. Each layer should be watered and then covered with 1/4" of soil. The grass clippings need to be loosened and scattered and mixed with a little soil. When the pile is finished, it should be covered with 1/2" or so of soil, or, in hot sunny climates, with hay to shade it. Once it is covered with something that is like a sheath or skin, the pile becomes what Rudolf Steiner called "an organism": it is an entity unto itself. It becomes part of the life of the Earth.

To insert the biodynamic preparations, take a rake handle or a pole and sink 5 holes evenly spaced around the pile, about 1' down in. The preparation can be mixed with damp earth, formed into a ball, and then pushed down into the pile. The hole should be closed up and then covered over. Stir the last preparation, the fermented Valerian juice, for 12 minutes or so in water in a glass jar. Then spray the liquid over the whole pile – beforehand, if you will be covering the pile with hay. A plastic spray bottle works quite well.

A compost pile can be built at any time of year. But people often make a compost pile in the fall after cleaning up the garden. If someone is building a pile gradually over a number of weeks, there is a biodynamic compost starter – dry – available from the Josephine Porter Institute. It is possible to take out a very small quantity – even half a teaspoon –, let it soak in water overnight, then stir it for a few minutes and sprinkle it on one or two layers of the pile. Valerian juice would also need to be ordered to spray on the pile when it is completed. (Sources for obtaining preparations will be given at the end of the chapter.)

The Earth is most alive and active internally from

fall to spring, especially in the winter. The heaped up compost pile in contact with the Earth takes part in the life cycle processes which go on within the Earth. Older biodynamic farmers sometimes bury their seeds in a box in the soil throughout the 12 Holy Nights from December 25 to January 6 (Epiphany, the Three Kings' Day, also the day when the Christ was baptized in the River Jordan). The farmers say that burying them for this period vitalizes the seeds. If the pile can be built in the fall and rest over the Winter, the period from November 15 to February 15, is also important. According to Rudolf Steiner, something happens in the Earth between January 15 and February 15, which is very helpful to the plants.

Where do the healing forces of biodynamics come from?

Many people assume that biodynamic practices are effective because of cosmic influences. It is true: The biodynamic method does help restore a connection with the cosmos which was slipping away, a connection with what comes to the plant from the sun and from the cosmos, though often in indirect ways. (The Nature Spirits have a great deal to do in mediating these processes.) Some of the cosmic influences are led to the plant as it goes through all kinds of complicated processes of growth and transformation. If plants are growing in sandy or stony soil, for example, they are much more readily influenced by light and by the cosmic aspects present within the compass of the earth. Whenever anything is rotting, however, and when a substantial amount of organic matter is present, then to a certain extent, the cosmic influences are shut out.

The living quality for which biodynamics is famous – both in the land itself and in what appears in the plants and animals – that living quality is carried particularly by all the organic processes: the partly digested quality of the manure supplied by the cow, the rotting plant material and manure in the compost pile, the compost spread out upon the Earth, and the sprouting, leafing plants growing up in the sunlight, air, and warmth. All of these processes take place over time around the cycle of the year. They are so complex that they cannot be really understood by science because not everything can be measured. The constant transformation and metamorphosis make it too difficult.

In the _Agriculture Course_ Rudolf Steiner emphasized at length that the re-enlivening of the Earth – to the extent that it is possible – takes place through **_processes of life_**. He observed,

> *"We must...provide for the true Nature-process to take place once more in the right way."*
>
> (Lecture 5)

> *"We must vitalize the earth directly, and this we cannot do by merely mineral procedures. [Aspects of cosmic influences connect to the mineral nature of the earth.] This we can only do by working with organic matter, bringing it into such a condition that it is able to organize and to vitalize the solid earthly element itself... this we can only do by bringing into the life of the plant such life as is already present on the Earth..."*
>
> (Lecture 5)

This life, he said, is "etherically living substance" (which people usually sense as vitality).

> *"Whatever is living,"* Rudolf Steiner added, *"must be kept within the living sphere. Ethereal*

39

life ... should never depart from anything that is in the sphere of living growth."

(Lecture 5)

"To manure the earth, is to make it alive..."

(Lecture 4)

In these modern times, nature can no longer be depended upon to give to the Earth enough decomposed organic residues. So, with compost, he said,

"We have a means of kindling the life within the earth it-self."

(Lecture 4)

"If such life [the organic processes] is also made use of in the plant's growth, the effect is to hold fast in the plant what is essentially earthly. The cosmic process works only in the stream which passes upward once more to seed-formation; while on the other hand the earthly process works in the unfolding of leaf, blossom, and so on, and the cosmic only radiates its influences into all this."

(Lecture 2)

In absolutely every process, the Nature Spirits are active. The undines are the great chemists working in all the more "earthly" processes of transformation; the sylphs store light and other influences in the air, and then approach the plants with them. Of the cow horn manure preparation 500 Rudolf Steiner said that it contains "an immense ethereal and astral force..."(Lecture 4). One remembers that the deep, rich prairie soils of the United States were built up by millions of buffalo, and that cattle have been sacred animals among many peoples.

40

Through the many varied nature processes, a middle sphere is created between heaven and the rocks below. This sphere is very thin, and our modern ways of living tend to make it even thinner and more inert. Biodynamics creates a much stronger, richer, more living middle realm.

What does it mean for the plant, for anything in the natural world to live in this middle sphere? Rudolf Steiner's descriptions are staggering in their implications: in a compost pile he said,

> "*the earthly material itself will tend to become inwardly alive – akin to the plant nature.*"
>
> (Lecture 4)

Many people sense this – some people have an absolutely extraordinary love and enthusiasm for compost. When we have added living forces to the manure through the preparations used in the compost pile, then, he said,

> "*[we endow] the plant itself with the power to receive into its body the influences which the soil contains.*"
>
> (Lecture 5)

It is as if each part of nature which contributes to these processes becomes more self-sufficient and independent, but in a cooperative way, in a way which contributes to the whole! He added,

> "*We must give [the manure] such a consistency that it will retain of its own accord as much nitrogen and other substances as it requires.*"
>
> (Lecture 5 – author's underlining)

He went even further in speaking of specific compost preparations. The effect of the stinging nettle preparation upon the soil:

> *"The soil will individualize itself in a nice relationship to the particular plants which you are growing. It is like a permeation of the soil with reason and with intelligence."*
>
> (Lecture 5)

The dandelion compost preparation:

> *"[It] will give the soil the faculty to attract just as much silicic acid from the atmosphere and from the cosmos as the plants need, to make them really sentient to all that is at work in their environment."*
>
> (Lecture 5)

The plant itself:

> *"will grow sensitive to all things and will draw to itself all that it needs."* It will be able to do this *"from a wide circle."*
>
> (Lecture 5)

This is extraordinary. The animals also become more self-sufficient. Everything becomes more and more independent, almost "free" in the way it composes itself, and more its true self. The whole landscape becomes more developed, and everything in it relates in a better way to everything else – the overall effect is very restorative.

Originally, biodynamic practices were used mainly in growing food and on pastures, but nature has declined so much in the past decade or two that it would now be important to do something for the land in general. A method has been developed for converting farms in India which is weaker than the original biodynamic method sketched out in the beginning of the chapter, but Peter Proctor from New Zealand, who has been helping the Indian farmers, says that it does seem to be working, although they would rather make compost by the original method if they could. Hundreds of farms have been converted, and 30% of all the vanilla now coming out of India is biodynamic.

The farmers in India are using CPP – a cow-pat-pit preparation (similar to barrel compost). It is easy to make the following simplified recipe: dig a hole about 1 1/2 feet deep and 2 feet by 2 feet square in the ground and line it with boards on the side – nothing on the bottom. (The hole could be longer.) Then take 2-3 buckets of cow manure (it needs to be fresh – perhaps cow pies gathered from a field). The cow manure can have a little bedding in it, not a lot. Mix it for 15-30 minutes on a tarp (or elsewhere) until it is completely aerated. Put it all in the pit, insert the biodynamic compost preparations about equidistant from one another halfway down into the manure, and sprinkle Valerian juice which has been stirred in water for 12 minutes or so onto the manure. The Valerian helps all the preparations to work together. (Whatever is left over can be sprinkled out on the ground.) Then a board should be put over the top as a cover and the manure allowed to rest over the winter until it turns into compost. Once finished, it needs to be stored in glass jars completely surrounded above, below, and on all sides with peat.

To use on the land, take about 1/2 cup of the simplified CPP preparation and stir it in a pail of water in alternating vortices for 12-20 minutes; then sprinkle or spray it out onto the land as a field spray. Since it needs to touch bare ground, the best time use it for lawns would be either when the grass has all died down in the fall or just before it begins to grow in the spring when there is still some bare earth showing between the clumps of grass. For a wood lot, it would be possible to sprinkle it around the woods or along paths, roads, or trails if the woods itself are too dense. Preparation 500, the cow manure spray, can be sprinkled out in the same way. It is different from the CPP preparation, which is a weaker compost treatment. Preparation 500 is an essential spray; it has to be stirred for an hour in alternating vortices without stopping. It will help whatever affects the root growth of the plant.

The quartz preparation 501 also needs to to be stirred in water for an hour without stopping in the same way in the morning. Equipment is necessary to spray it on foliage in larger areas, although a plastic spray bottle would work for most lawns. For fruit trees or extensive spraying, a backpack sprayer will be necessary, with a special nozzle which can spray 20' or more. Generally, the spray should be a fine mist. For taller trees, however, one can shoot a coarser stream of spray above the tree on a breezy day and let the wind shatter it into a mist. For wood lots, 501 could be sprayed on ground plants and shrubs because these will carry the right influences into the soil even if one can't spray the trees. The best time would be before the plants flower, since the cosmic influences appear more as the plants reach the flowering stage. A stirred spray preparation remains viable for 2 – 3 hours.

For dry regions where the soil is very thin, it may be necessary to create a more sheltered environment with its own microclimate, within stands of brush or trees, or in the midst of buildings, for example. The environment can be very intense where sky meets earth and where there is not so much in the middle. People in desert areas using biodynamic practices will be creating a new environment!

One set of biodynamic compost preparations can be used for up to 15 cubic yards of material. However, even a small backyard compost pile still needs one set of preparations. The preparations should be stored in peat, surrounded on all sides and above and below in glass jars if they are going to be kept for some time. The quartz preparation can be left on a windowsill in the sun if it is away from electrical wires and outlets.

The biodynamic method may seem very complicated at first. Once one has become used to it, however, it is not difficult at all. People become much more aware of what they are doing and of how nature responds. The whole landscape becomes more alive, and gentler.

Sources for obtaining information and preparations

Biodynamic Farming and Gardening Association
25844 Butler Road
Junction City, OR 97448
541-998-0105
www.biodynamics.com

- Books and information.
- A good reference for bees: *Toward Saving the Honeybee* by Gunther Hauk.
- Information about local biodynamic groups and conferences

Josephine Porter Institute for Applied Biodynamics
P.O. Box 133
Woolwine, VA 24185-0133
276-930-2463
www.jpibiodynamics.org

- Compost preparations
- Barrel Compost
- Field Spray
- Preparations 500 and 501

Oregon Biodynamic Group
503-635-3941
www.oregonbd.org

- Good website
- Contact number for preparations and barrel compost

Biodynamic training programs

Rudolf Steiner College
9200 Bannister Road
Fair Oaks, CA 95628
916-961-8727
www.steinercollege.edu

The Pfeiffer Center
260 Hungry Hollow Rd.
Chestnut Ridge, NY 10977
845-352-5020
www.pfeiffercenter.org

4

HOW DO WE AFFECT THE NATURE SPIRITS THROUGH WHO WE ARE?

One of the people who understood the Nature Spirits quite well and their relationship to human beings was William Shakespeare. The fairy kingdom has a major part in his play *A Midsummer Night's Dream.*

Once upon a time, Midsummer Night was the main festival of the year. Rudolf Steiner described it in several of his lecture courses. The wonderful singing of the birds in spring and early summer is not simply a means to communicate with other birds or a way of claiming territory. The rising up through the atmosphere of the earth of all these many, many bird songs, sounding far out into the heavens, is actually a gift to the cosmos. Later in the course of the year, the music, now something we no longer hear, resounds back to the birds, filled with the wisdom of the cosmos. It is a means of insight for them. Human beings are developing a more particular, individual consciousness. In very humble creatures – for example, a fish – there is something of a much more universal awareness.

` During the midsummer festivals of the past, people celebrated with songs and dances, they enacted dramatic stories and read poetry, which rose up into the heavens just as the birds gave up their songs to the cosmos. Something of the human being went upward too, and in that state people were penetrated for a short time by their higher moral nature.

Times have changed. Because we have evolved further, our higher self is more likely to become manifest now in midwinter, at Christmas, when the world leaves us more to ourselves, when we are alone with ourselves. Then the higher self has the possibility of being born in us. Midsummer now is often a time when people go out and are active in the world, traveling, learning, experiencing, working. People can also "go out of themselves" spiritually, in a kind of soul exhilaration. It can become an intoxication with the freedom of summer, a disruption of someone's true being and life, and that is what happens in Shakespeare's play.

The story takes place at a ducal palace with a forest nearby, a forest inhabited by fairies. When the audience first sees the fairies and their King and Queen, they are beautiful, wonderful, bearing much grace and majesty. But then things start to deteriorate. The King and Queen are experiencing marital conflicts, and the King has a mischievous spirit place a potion on the eyes of the Queen while she sleeps so that she will fall in love with the first creature she sees when she awakens. She falls in love with a clown wearing a donkey's head.

The Duke is on the verge of marrying Hippolyta, the Queen of the Amazons. A young woman of his court named Hermia wants to marry her love, a young man named Lysander, but her rigid and rigorous father wants her to marry another, Demetrius, or he will invoke an ancient law and have her put to death! She and Lysander escape into the forest, followed by Demetrius and by another woman, Helena, who loves Demetrius. In most true fairy tales, the forest is a place of embroilment where people become lost, where they cannot see where they are going, and where they may lose what they are.

Shakespeare seems to have known what the fairies – the Nature Spirits – need today. They need people to know who they are themselves, why they are here, who they are supposed to be with and what they are supposed to be doing. If people are, in a sense, lost, then the fairy kingdom comes into disorder, and the disorders aggravate one another, which is exactly what happens in the play. The potion also gets put on the eyes of Lysander as he lies asleep beside his love Hermia in the forest – it is put there by mistake. He is awakened by Helena, looking for her love Demetrius who has scorned her and who wants to marry Lysander's Hermia. As soon as Lysander awakens, the potion takes effect and he immediately falls madly in love with Helena. He abandons the sleeping Hermia and runs through the forest pursuing Helena. All the relationships erupt into quarrels.

The people in the play need to find their true relationships – and themselves – and until it happens, everything is chaos. Finally the spell is broken, and the fairy Queen and the deluded Lysander are released from their enchantment. Each finds his own love again, and Demetrius realizes that Helena was meant to be his true love. The fairy King and Queen are reconciled, and the smaller fairies become quiet and human again, instead of blowing about like gusts of wind. When the lovers go back to the palace where Demetrius will implore Hermia's father to allow her to marry Lysander whom she loves, the Duke is ready himself to marry Hippolyta the next day. He agrees that on the morrow, he and his love and the two younger couples will all be married in one ceremony! So they retire to the palace to sleep.

Then comes the scene which is so telling. What happens is not exactly in the words of the play, but every director in the six or so productions I have seen over decades has understood the final scene in the same way. The people go into the palace to sleep. (Today the higher self, or even the Christ Impulse can come in during sleep, depending upon how we have lived while awake.) The fairies steal into the palace and congregate kneeling in the hall on the first floor, and they bless the sleeping human beings. The mood is one of awe, and of hope. The fact that the human beings have found themselves and their right path brings hope to the fairies, and as the play closes, it is as if they are waiting for something. We don't know what it is, but the hope is almost tangible. It is like a promise of a new world.

The inner state of human beings means a great deal to the world. The Nature Spirits have invisible bodies which exist on the level of our general state of vitality (what is "etheric" in us) or on the level of our feelings and ordinary thoughts (what is "astral.") These invisible aspects of ourselves are real to them, and they can be affected by them. Any single human being, or any group will have an effect on the whole surrounding area, depending upon how they live their lives.

There is a striving in nature. If we look, for example, at the trees in winter when the leaves have fallen away, if we live in places where that happens, it is possible to see that every tree has its own gesture. They all strive upward, but differently. It is very moving to look out into the plant world and to see how each kind tries to strive upwards.

Adam Bittleston, a Christian Community priest, described an experience he had had one morning.

> *"On a clear, sunny autumn morning, I had walked into the gardens of St. John's College, Oxford. The dahlias were still in bloom and the Michaelmas daisies were covered with great butterflies – tortoise shells, fritillaries, and red admirals. Suddenly I saw the whole scene take on a new figure; every plant assumed a different and intelligible pattern, an individuality with a mean-*

ing that was the plant itself, which by existing in that pattern was turned towards God and was praising Him! So with the butterflies; they were not merely lowly organisms but intensely alive, clad in the livery of God, and in a fashion more personal than the plants were praising Him too. The world was a prayer...."

The plant world "remembers" the creative working of the spiritual worlds and expresses what for the human being would be intent and will through its forms and through its seeking of the light.

Yet, the nature world cannot quite reach the angelic world. Over long ages, an outpouring of love from the Godhead and from the hierarchies brought about the creation of the world. Two thousand years ago this love was given over to human beings. It is now something which can develop in people over time through the Christ Impulse. This great change is implicit; it stands as background behind the ending of Shakespeare's *A Midsummer Night's Dream*. The fairies very likely did not know exactly why they were blessing the human beings, and why they felt such hope. But there is good reason for that hope if we can live into our destiny. The nature world is incomplete – it needs something – something which comes to a lesser degree from the human being now, but which will become much more definitive over the course of the coming millennia.

There is a new spiritual quality developing out of human beings which will fructify the world. It is based upon the inner transformation we go through as we become better human beings. The following passage is from the last lecture in Rudolf Steiner's lecture cycle on *The Gospel of St. Luke*.

"When a man's whole being is pervaded with the love that streamed from the cross on Golgotha, he can turn his eyes to the future and say: evolution on the earth must make it possible for the spirit living within me gradually to transform the whole of earth existence. We shall in time give back again to the Father-principle... the spirit we have received; we shall let our whole being be permeated with the Christ principle and our hands will bring to expression what is living in our souls as a faithful picture of the Father principle, and the Christ principle will stream through them... so that the outer world will be eventually imbued with the Christ principle."

This will be the role of the human being: to transform the world spiritually through the love he can develop in his own being.

There are simple things we can do now. The saying of Grace is actually very important. Even when people are not aware of the role the Nature Spirits play in helping the plant world, the appreciation and gratitude which people feel for the food which sustains them matters. When we eat vegetables, for example, it is not the same as when an animal eats the plants. The higher angelic hierarchies, the normally developed ones, now have a relationship to the faculties which constitute our inner being; our capacities to think, to feel, to will to do things, to perceive with our senses, and to remember. Christianity, and most religions, work at the purification and the development of these capacities. When animals eat plants, when the plants pass into their systems, because of the horizontal spine of the animal, Rudolf Steiner says, spiritually the plants are cast back upon the Earth. (*Man as Symphony of the Creative Word*, Lecture 11, November 10,1923.) The animals have considerable fear in them – this can often be seen if one observes closely, and this fear is cast back. When the plant passes into us, on the other hand, we liberate and spiritualize the plants so that what is liberated from them strives upward to the hierarchies. The Nature Spirits, the elemental beings, are all closely connected to this process.

The blessing of the meal is quite a significant act, because in our consciousness it establishes a bridge upward. There would be no material, no substance of any kind, if invisible elemental beings had not allowed themselves to be enchanted into rigidity so that something solid or liquid could come into being. Wherever we can see or touch something, invisible beings had to make a sacrifice. It matters to them greatly if, as we live our lives, we know that. When we eat the food, we liberate them, and they need what is present in our consciousness as a bridge leading toward the angelic hierarchies.

Rudolf Steiner gave a grace which hints at the correspondences: what takes place in nature, and what takes place in us.

The plant seeds quicken in the night of the earth,
The young shoots are growing through the power of the air,
And all fruits are ripening through the might of the sun.

So quickens the soul in the shrine of the heart,
So emerges the power of spirit in the light of the world,
So ripens human strength in the glory of God.

If we do not progress in our own development, then nature is left to decline, to sink lower and lower.

One can understand even better how the human being is now called to lead, out of his own being, from sentences which Rudolf Steiner gave in 1923 as preparation for a meditation. The meditation begins: "I gaze into the darkness. In it arises Light – Living Light." It speaks of preparing for the discovery of the true self. The following lines were given as a preparatory meditation.

> *The <u>stones</u> are mute; I have placed and hidden the eternal creator word in them; chaste and modest they hold it in the depths.*

> Materia prima. <u>Matter hardens in itself.</u>

> *The <u>plants</u> live and grow. I have placed the eternal creator word in them; sprouting and thriving they carry it into the depths.*
> M. Secunda. <u>Matter opens itself to the spirit.</u>

> *The <u>animals</u> feel and will. I have placed the eternal creator word in them; shaping and moulding they hold it in the depths.*

> M. Tertia. <u>Matter shines in the light of the soul.</u>

> *The <u>human being</u> thinks and acts; I have placed the eternal creator word in him; he should fetch it from the depths.*

> Spiritus Tertius. <u>The I finds itself in the world.</u>

> *The <u>soul</u> knows and is devoted; I shall release my eternal creator word from her, that she may carry it into the heights of purity and piety.*

Spiritus Secundus. <u>The I sacrifices itself to God.</u>

The <u>spirit</u> releasing itself loves the Universe. I speak in it my eternal creator word, awakening and liberating the world in purity.

Spiritus Primus. <u>The I works in God.</u>

From the *Collected Works, Vol. 265,* V.S., translator.

The human being is not his physical body; our body is constantly being renewed, cell by cell, as long as we live. What is constant are the invisible aspects of ourselves which maintain this form. If the higher aspects of ourselves change for the better, then something of that metamorphosis may appear in the body as it is continually renewed. The French lithographer of the 19th century, Honoré Daumier, was acutely aware of this. His newspaper prints – satires of various public figures of his time – revealed immediately the significance of the ethical and moral changes people go through which express themselves in the body. Most of Daumier's observations were of negative effects. But, there can also be positive changes.

> *"If we had many opportunities in life of showing friendliness and kindness," Rudolf Steiner said, "Nature is inclined, as soon as this kindness has been expressed in the countenance, to receive it into her own essential being."*

If we have been permeated by an inclination to live out of kindness, permeated so strongly that it affects our physical features, then Nature itself begins to absorb that quality from us! This is quite startling.

But that isn't all. He continued:

"Nature takes our memories into her forces, our gestures into her very being. The human being is so intimately connected with external nature that there is immense significance for the latter in the memories he experiences in his soul and also in the way in which he expresses his inner life of soul in physiognomy and gesture."

Mystery Knowledge and Mystery Centers
(Nov. 25, 1923)

As one might expect, we can also have a negative influence. Our feelings, our memories, the effects of our thoughts, everything we want to do, everything that makes its way into our thoughts is all taken up by the hierarchies at night when we sleep. They reject, however, everything immoral and send it back to the earth – into us. And, somehow, the earth receives all the immorality which is rejected. One can look at Shakespeare's play *Macbeth* with all the storms and darkness which appear because of the murders Macbeth commits. This is not pure imagination.

"To be immoral," Rudolf Steiner said, 'means, 'To withdraw from the Earth the seeds of life.' "

Rudolf Steiner commented:

"The all-essential causes of what happens on the earth do not lie outside man; they lie within mankind."

Nearly every religion tries to cope with this problem, by concentrating upon improving human nature.

"The destiny," he said, "of our physical earth-planet in another 2,000 years will not depend upon the present constitution of our mineral world, but upon what we do and allow to be done. With world-consciousness, human responsibility widens into world responsibility."

(Lecture of November 9, 1919)

One remembers the old retired people: As people age, they often lose the roughness of their personality, they tend to live more in interest and in appreciation, and they have time to take care of things. The atmosphere of homes and gardens belonging to older people is often rare and wonderful.

It would not be impossible for the rest of us too to become stewards of humanity and of the world. In the hard times coming, a complete change of culture will become necessary if we are to keep hope and goodness alive and strong. The number of projects possible would be enormous: schools, camps, individuals, groups of people taking something up on their days off, businesses, organizations, people in rehabilitation – there is an enormous amount that could be done wherever an individual or a group has a constructive interest: in fact, the variety of interests is very important. We are really the tenth angelic hierarchy – we still have a long way ahead of us. But even what we are capable of now, however humble, matters.

There is something quite simple which we don't think about: even the way we <u>see</u> matters. Rudolf Steiner described his high school chemistry teacher:

"He had quite extraordinary eyes. They looked out into the world in such a way that you felt: he sees everything in Nature, and everything in Nature enters into him through his look. It all goes

*into his look, and his look rays it out again; he
has it there in him."*

He mentioned this man in Chapter 2 of his Autobiography. Why would this be so significant? Because we establish unconsciously a relationship with the elemental beings enchanted into substance wherever we look, and this relationship can be crucial to them. We don't know how significant seemingly insignificant things can be.

The Nature Spirits are spiritually "upside down". Their bodies are invisible because they are on a "higher" level than the physical level where we can see, but their consciousness is down on the physical level, or even lower. We are the opposite: our bodies are there on the physical level, but our consciousness is much higher: we are oriented "upward", so to speak. The Nature Spirits bring substance into manifestation out of the spiritual. They have worked like this, worked at an end-task of creation, for a long, long time.

The higher hierarchies who worked for so long throughout all the stages of creation completed their earlier tasks, and now they have others. They leave human beings in freedom now, but they have a new relationship to us through our own human faculties, depending upon how we use them. This includes our sense perception. The angelic beings who used to inspire thoughts into people more than 2,000 years ago now weave between us and our sense perceptions. They don't try to determine anything in us, but there is a relationship.

How we use our soul faculties – sense perception, memory, thinking, feeling, willing – what our interests are, and the quality of how we live actively through these faculties, all of this is important. Rudolf Steiner didn't say exactly how we form a bridge, but apparently once we have looked at something, especially if we can think that elemental beings lie there fixed into rigidity, and that all of them have tasks without which the world couldn't exist, then they stay connected to us, and when we die, they can find the rightful angelic beings again. Without us, they could come under the sway of fallen beings.

Two hints of how people are related now to the hierarchies: how we speak is important. If we speak well and say significant things, true things, then we come into a connection with the archangelic world during sleep. It can be a good idea to read poetry out loud during the day, since our ordinary talking may not have been adequate to make a connection possible!

Another hint: in one particular lecture, Rudolf Steiner described what a seer perceives, looking at someone lying asleep on a bed. Inside, inside the human being, on the inward side of the senses, a gently glowing light, growing more and more strong, moves glowing into the sleeping human being from behind the senses. The light has to do with angelic beings, and the degree to which this happens has to do with the use we made of our senses while we were awake, during the day.

5

THE IMPORTANCE OF SPIRITUAL
UNDERSTANDING TODAY

*"[Our] soul provides the stage upon which the
world itself begins to experience its own evolution and existence."*
                    Rudolf Steiner, An Autobiography
                                        (Chapter 22)

Evolution never stands still, and everything is always developing and changing. For that reason, the
whole world outlook which a human being holds is very
significant. The Nature Spirits are offspring of the angelic hierarchies. They work at the manifestation and the
dissolution of substance, and many of them have gladly
allowed themselves to be enchanted into rigidity so that
substance could arise: substance which supports all of us,
in one way or another, for our life on earth. In a number
of places, it is quite clear from Rudolf Steiner's indica-
tions that the Nature Spirits are in danger of not being
able to find their way back into a connection with the angelic hierarchical beings. The more we permeate the
earth and its atmosphere with what Rudolf Steiner called
sub-nature forces – electricity, magnetism, radiation –
then the more the earth environment becomes a habitat
for the wrong kinds of beings, and the more conscious we

need to be of what it takes to create a healthy environment. This includes the thought and feeling environment we provide, because the elemental beings know what we think and feel. In addition, he predicted that at the end of the twentieth century, "a new spring" of nature beings would arise, Nature Spirits connected with the Christ. That was to occur about 100 years after the end of Kali Yuga (1899), the period of spiritual darkening which had lasted approximately 5,000 years. It is significant that the Christ Being came in toward the middle of that time. Yet, as one looks around the world, especially if one is old enough to compare what the world is now with the way it was even 40 years ago, to sustain whatever is good, we will need to be ready to create or restore it ourselves. In a way, it is as if we have been living in a kind of Garden of Eden where everything was given to us, more or less. Now it needs our work and help.

In earlier times, if changes needed to be made, people called directly upon higher beings to make those changes. In our time, however, what Rudolf Steiner called the original Divine-Spiritual-Creator-Beings, the angelic hierarchies who worked to bring about the creation on behalf of the Godhead mediated by the Christ who was then working out of the heavenly world, have taken new tasks: they are connected now to our use of our human faculties. One can see this change if one looks at the difference between Christianity and more ancient spiritual practices. The emphasis has shifted from what was going on in the heavens to the moral condition and the moral will of the human being. That connection becomes effective when we work very hard: when we try to think the right things and to discover what would be best to do; when we try to discover the right feelings which can bring us and everything else forward. There needs to be whole-hearted human striving in this direction (and time to rest to let things mature also).

In the version in Hebrew of the story of Creation in Genesis, one word occurs over and over again: Elohim. It is translated as "God". But the –im ending is plural. The Elohim are the most highly developed of one of the angelic hierarchies, the Spirits of Form. The following are the angelic hierarchies:

The Godhead	The Father God
	The Son God
	The Holy Spirit
1st hierarchy	The Seraphim (Spirits of Love)
	The Cherubim (Spirits of Harmony and Wisdom)
	The Thrones (Spirits of Will)
2nd hierarchy	The Kyriotetes (Spirits of Wisdom)
	The Dynameis (Spirits of Movement)
	The Exusiai (Spirits of Form, including Elohim)
3rd hierarchy	The Archai (Spirits of Time)
	The Archangels (Spirits of Fire)
	The Angels (Sons of Twilight)
10th hierarchy	human beings

If one looks from the Godhead down through the different angelic hierarchies, one can see the progression from love on down toward the human being – the progression of creation. The Kyriotetes are those angelic beings who know fully what comes from the Godhead and the highest hierarchies. Part of their role is to communicate that to the Spirits of Movement and to the Spirits of Form. If spirits are fallen, then they are no longer part of this communication, and they become advocates for what they knew in the past, or for other things.

The Spirits of Form, at very early stages of creation, sacrificed to us what was to become our physical body, then our etheric (the vitality one can sense), then our astral (where our feelings and most of our thoughts live), and finally they sacrificed to us what has become the substance of the core of our higher being. During the period before the Christ incarnated, their tasks had changed, and they were inspiring thoughts into people. This changed again, Rudolf Steiner said, in the fourth century A.D. when the Exusiai, the Spirits of Form, gave up that task (which now leaves us free to think our own thoughts). Now these beings weave between us and what we see.

This has enormous significance, because human beings have had such an important relationship for so long to these beings (included among them, the Elohim). The Nature Spirits bring form into manifestation so that it can be seen. This might be why it is so important for us to be conscious of the Nature Spirits' role when we look at whatever we see in the natural world. It may be that we help to make a bridge again to the original Creator Beings through the use of our consciousness when we look. Then perhaps it can actually provide a means of salvation almost for the nature beings. There may be other reasons why it is important to think of the Nature Spirits when we look. But knowing that the Spirits of Form are present when we see, and that we also form a connection to the Nature Spirits does at least alert us to the fact that things which we take for granted – just looking at the grass, for example – might be far more important than we know, depending upon how we do it, or upon what our outlook is.

There is a passage in Rudolf Steiner's lecture _Man as Symphony of the Creative Word_, where the Nature

Spirits try to give advice to the human being. The message they bring, said Rudolf Steiner,

> is "the World-Word [sounding] forth from the concordance of these countless beings."
>
> (Lecture 9)

The chorus of elemental beings addresses the human being with strong admonitions.

The Chorus of Earth Spirits (Gnomes):
> Strive to awaken.

The Chorus of Water Spirits (Undines):
> Think in the spirit.

The Chorus of Air Spirits (Sylphs):
> Live creatively breathing existence.

The Chorus of Fire Spirits (Salamanders):
> Receive in love the Will-power of
> the Gods.

It sounds like very good advice. But do these admonitions mean to them what we would mean if we said those words?

Actually, they are asking, it turns out, that we see everything, that we see ourselves as they understand us.

> "When the gnome-chorus allows its 'Strive to awaken' to sound forth," said Rudolf Steiner, "this – only transformed into gnome language – is the force which is active in bringing about the human bony system, the system of movement in general."
>
> (Lecture 9)

"Strive to awaken," means to them "perceive what produces the skeleton!" Gnomes work in the mineral world, with what is hard. The driest and most intellectual of our thoughts are bone-thinking; these thoughts are spiritually related to our bones, they are like the thinking of the gnomes.

What is the force they are talking about?

"In our souls," said Rudolf Steiner, "we actually possess the predisposition to human love, and to that warmth which understands the other man. In the solid components of our organism, however, we bear moral cold. This is the force which from the spiritual worlds, welds, as it were our physical organism together."

(Lecture 12, November 11, 1923, p. 209)

If we were "to awaken" in this way, and to identify ourselves spiritually with what brought about the bony system, then the forces we would meet would be moral cold and lack understanding!

"The bone," said Rudolf Steiner, "leads man astray into hatred."

Rudolf Steiner's explanations of the other admonitions of the Nature Spirits:

"When the undines utter 'think in the spirit' they utter – transposed into the undine sphere – what pours itself as world word into man in order to give form to the organs of digestion."

"When the sylphs, as they are breathed in, allow their 'Live creatively breathing existence' to stream downwards, there penetrates into man, weaving and pulsating through him, the force

which endows him with the organs of the rhythmic system."

(Lecture 9, November 4, 1923, p.163)

The admonition of the Fire-Spirits " Receive in love the Will-Power of the Gods," has to do with the creation of our system of nerves, the deadest part of ourselves. Everything in the message conveyed by the elemental sprits has to do with the creation of the human body in substance, and much of it very likely took place before birth. They 'know' us through what they themselves normally do in performance of their tasks.

Is what they say a characterization of our true being? It really isn't. We are a soul-spiritual being. They are describing our physical body and how it was created.

It should now be possible to see at once how important it is for us and for the world if we are able to hold in consciousness all of what Rudolf Steiner communicated about the human being:

the present task of the human being;

the whole history of earth evolution given in his book *An Outline of Esoteric Science;*

the understanding of the human being in spirit, soul, and body given in his book *Theosophy*;

the process of higher development, including the strengthening, purification, and metamorphosis of the human faculties described in *How to Know Higher Worlds* and other works;

the changes brought about by the Incarnation of the Christ Being;

and the role of the human being in the future evolution of the Earth.

If we are truly to awaken, it means to be able to face the natural world knowing who we are as soul-spirit beings. To be able to "think in the spirit", we need to know what spirit is, which Rudolf Steiner characterized over and over again in _Theosophy_. It doesn't, for us, mean the creation of the body. It was in earlier epochs that people were able to find a direct connection to the spiritual world through breathing – now it comes more through thinking, "breathing light." In earlier epochs people asked to receive the will of God into themselves, whereas now we have to develop that out of ourselves, out of our interests, and out of the sense of task we brought from before birth, out of our ideals, our spiritual knowledge, our connection to the Christ Impulse.

Through the chorus of the elemental beings, we can hear and imagine what worked through creation in all the earlier epochs and which has come to an end in the natural world, but we also need to have a clear awareness of what is to develop out of our inner nature - the love, for example, which was one of the "forces" or "strengths" which the Christ brought to the Earth. This we need to develop, and it can then permeate not only the Earth, but those parts of the cosmos which have grown, in Rudolf Steiner's words, "frosty cold".

In the last lecture of _Karmic Relationships_, Volume III, Rudolf Steiner gave a very significant picture of a council of archangels which made a decision about 1200 years ago to try to make the earth more dependent upon the cosmos, the original source of the forces the elemental beings were speaking about. That inspiration is active everywhere. But, he said, it was an error: the archangels were worried about deteriorating conditions on the sun, which manifest for us in sunspot storms. Because they didn't know what else to do, they forsook the path of the Christ and that of the Archangel Michael. Michael was known for centuries all over Europe and the Middle East as the Sun Archangel, the Archangel who always worked on behalf of God the Father, and then, on behalf of the Christ.

The understanding which human beings can win through spiritual study is crucial, not only for themselves, but also for every invisible being above and around them. In an important lecture given on October 10, 1916, "How Can the Soul Needs of the Time Be Met?" Rudolf Steiner described the conditions under which the angelic beings now live:

> *"For men who live here on the Earth, it is right to say: With the mystery of Golgotha, Christ entered earthly life and is since then present in earthly life. From a certain point of view it can be felt as a source of happiness for earthly life, that Christ has entered into it. But if one puts oneself into the point of view of the Angels (and this point of view is no invention of mine, for this point of view is found as something quite real by the true spiritual researcher), the Angels in their spiritual sphere experienced it differently; they experienced the opposite. Christ has gone from their realm to men, He left their realm. For themselves, they have to say: Through the Mystery of Golgotha Christ has departed from our world. They have reason to be as sad about this, as men can feel it is for their salvation that Christ has come to them, as dwellers in a physical body.*
>
> *This sequence of thought is real; one who truly understands the spiritual world knows that there is only one salvation for the Angels, for whom what I have just expressed is correct, and that is that men on Earth in their physical bodies so live with the thought of Christ that the thought of Christ shines up as a light to the Angels, since the time of the Mystery of Golgotha. Men say: Christ has entered our being, and we can develop ourselves in such a way that He lives within us: "Not I, but the Christ in me." But the Angels say:*

For our realm Christ has departed from our inner being, and shines up to us like many stars in the Christ-filled thought of individual men; there we recognize Him again, from thence He shines up to us since the Mystery of Golgotha. It is a real relationship between the spiritual world and the human world.

This real relationship is expressed in this way too, that the spiritual beings inhabiting the spiritual world outside us, look with happiness and satisfaction and recognition at the thoughts which we are able to form about their world. They can only help us when we are able to form thoughts about them, even though we have not reached the point of being able to look clairvoyantly into the spiritual world. They can help us, if we know about them."

The author has not discovered whether Rudolf Steiner would have said that people also need to hold an understanding of the Christ for the Nature Spirits – but it is very likely. They live in an in-between realm where it is possible they could encounter other beings claiming to be the Christ. The Christ is a help to the Nature Spirits, but whether they are consciously aware of exactly who He is, I don't know. The following is one of the versions of the Foundation Stone Meditation which Rudolf Steiner brought to the members of the Anthroposophical Society at the Christmas Conference when it was founded:

Light Divine	Göttliches Licht,
Christ-Sun	Christus-Sonne
The Spirits of the Elements	Das Hören die Ele-
hear it....	mentar Geister…

"Elementar Geister" has been translated as "the spirits of the Elements" but the Elementar Geister are actually spirits of the Sun, "elementary spirits"; they are higher beings than the Nature Spirits. So it is possible that the Nature Spirits do not really know the Christ, and that what the human beings in their vicinity understand is crucial for them.

We can say a grace whenever we partake of food. The elemental beings enchanted into the food will be dissolved and freed, and our thoughts, our knowledge, and our convictions will be there to act as a bridge for them. We can live side by side with them. They will know what we think and feel, and we will provide an environment for them, just as through their work, they help provide an environment for us.

People have sometimes complained that those who mainly study Rudolf Steiner's works aren't doing anything for the world. It isn't true. When people can come to an understanding of what is true about the human being and the spiritual world today, light which we can't see pours into the world – the world grows lighter and more humane.

There is much to be done to help the world, and many ways to do it. We do not work for ourselves alone.

6

A POSTLUDE: BEETHOVEN'S NINTH SYMPHONY

When Rudolf Steiner was a young man in his twenties, in the process of editing Goethe's scientific works, an artist whom he knew went about from person to person taking a survey of notable people, which he later published in a little booklet. Many of the questions were normal ones: What do you like most about men? What do you like most about women? What is your favorite food? Some of the questions were more profound – for example, what would you be most likely to forgive? To the question: who is your favorite composer?, Rudolf Steiner answered, Beethoven.

What could this possibly have to do with the subject of this book?

An answer is there in Beethoven's last symphony, the Ninth Symphony, which he wrote at the end of his life, when he had become so profoundly deaf that he couldn't hear it except in his imagination, and when he had become so deeply disillusioned with humanity that he was a trial to live with for his best friends. He cast all of that aside long enough to write an extraordinary and exceptionally original work.

The theme of the first movement is creation: the creation of the universe, the creation of the world. It is a huge, complex, sublime creation – seemingly chaotic. Short descending motifs flash through the orchestra like streaks of lightening – it is as if the whole universe is seething in the act of bringing about creation. The Nature Spirits belong to the theme of creation. As the servants of the hierarchies and the Christ, who worked among them in the heavens, they made everything here below visible.

The second movement is almost pure forward-plummeting energy with a certain repetitive quality to it and much banging on the tympani. The Ninth Symphony was quite a prophetic work, because in the twentieth century in particular, this forward explosion of energy was becoming more and more obvious as a spiritual force. Some of the early commentators who wrote about Beethoven's Ninth Symphony considered the second movement to be diabolic. Energy like this has become so much a part of modern life that today, generally, people probably find it stimulating. But in the relentless, pounding forward rush, something is missing, in fact, a great deal.

The Nature Spirits have consciousness and feeling, but they do not have an "I". In Rudolf Steiner's work, the "I" is called the Ego, which is the Latin word for I. People know it mostly as the lower, distorted aspect of the self – as what is present in egoism. But, the ego is really the core of our being; it is what brings in and what will bear the higher self. It is the hidden self which masters and transforms the lower aspects of ourselves.

The first word which designates something like the core of an individual, the "Self" which makes decisions and which can become truly morally responsible, appeared in a play by the Greek Tragedian Euripides in the fifth century B.C. If one goes back to the poems of the Greek poet Homer, to _The Iliad_ (the Trojan War) and _The Odyssey_, which were written down earlier in the 700s B.C., one notices that when a person needed to make a major decision, a god or goddess would appear, either visibly or invisibly, and tell him what needed to be done. It was a period when thoughts were inspired into people. Solon, the famous law-giver of Athens, was asked to become head of the Athenian City State in the 600s B.C. for exactly that reason: he was an inspired poet and philosopher.

According to Rudolf Steiner, the substance of the human ego was brought into incarnation long, long before recorded history. The ego has been developing ever since. But people began to become conscious of it, of being able to live in it, only between approximately 600-400 B.C., shortly (historically speaking) before the incarnation of the Christ.

The Nature Spirits do not have an ego – that is why they are vulnerable. Our ego in part lives in the periphery – it was once more firmly in the body. Now, it lives in our interest, in our sense for our tasks, in our love and understanding, in our struggles to find the right path in the higher aspects of ourselves, in our relation to destiny.

In the Ninth Symphony, the first movement had to do with the creation, the second with an onward-plunging energy, energy for the sake of energy, forward propulsion for the sake of rushing forward. The third movement to the symphony is very different. Beethoven said it was "man" – the human being.

The mood is entirely different from the other two movements. It begins in a way which is quiet, barely formed, and, in a way, not capable. The theme is very undeveloped. It does seem to be conscious of itself, and it tries to go forward, but it tends to peter out after a very short time, and there is a breath, a hesitation, a gap. Then it starts again and evolves a little further, and then ceases. Another gap. This goes on for some time. But the quality of the gaps and hesitations changes: it becomes ever clearer that something more will come before long, and that it will be greater and finer than what has gone before. The themes become more and more developed, many voices breaking off and going somewhere else but supporting, others joining or taking over for short intervals. And then, suddenly, the melody breaks forth and begins to sing and sing, weaving and traversing many registers, melodies weaving about melodies, until it seems as if it will never end. It is like something learning how to live out of consciousness and love in a way that was almost impossible for it in the beginning. (It is possible to play this movement oneself from a piano score – it is also a good piano piece.)

Then comes the famous fourth movement based on Friedrich Schiller's "Ode to Joy", a hymn to human brotherhood. The orchestra tries to introduce the theme, but fragments like left-over inclinations from the first movement occupy the sound-space, and they refuse to let anything happen. Alarming motifs from the creation movement, and others which are more extreme mechanical versions of it, break in and stop the true theme of the fourth movement and almost crush it out of existence. Finally, when it seems as if the new main theme is going to be overwhelmed and crushed, for the first time in the history of symphonic music, a single human voice breaks in and stops everything – "No! Not these sounds!" – and silences the interruptions. The voice begins to sing alone the true theme for the fourth movement, the theme from Schiller's Ode. Then his voice is joined by others, and together, the orchestra, the soloists, and an immense chorus are able to develop it on and on in unimagined ways.

The "Ode to Joy" is an Ode to Brotherhood.

On what is this brotherhood based? It seems to come out of a consciousness, an over-welling love and constructiveness, a sense for human values, a confidence in them and a willingness to carry them forward – where people, with no compulsion whatsoever, join and go forward based on human values in which they all know they can live. Today many individuals, in differing circumstances, will be that voice. It was a prophetic work, and it pointed to a way for the future.

About the Author

Elizabeth (Beth) Wieting was born in Virginia in 1942 and raised in Massachusetts. She grew up in an extended family who appreciated nature. In 1965 a move to Oregon introduced her to the volcanic wilderness of the Northwest. Living in the city of Portland, before organic food was available, she grew much of her family's fruit and vegetables in the back yard! During that time she devel oped an appreciation for the contribution of the Nature Spirits to our world.

Beth was a high school humanities and foreign language teacher for 23 years. She also served as a board member of the Biodynamic Farming and Gardening Association from 1985 - 1995 and was its Vice President from 1990 - 1995. As an environmental activist and lobbyist in 1969 - 1971, Beth was Chairperson for the Oregon/ Southern Washington Coalition for Clean Air, which was responsible for carrying the enabling legislation for the 1970 Clean Air Act. She also served as a board member for the Northwest Environmental Defense Center.

The author has given lectures and workshops on biodynamics for over 20 years throughout the United States and Canada.